SCAN THE QR CODE TO CHECK OUT VOLUME 1 OF 250 UNUSUAL FACTS TO LEARN ON THE LOO

SCAN ME

RUBBER BANDS WILL LAST MUCH LONGER WHEN THEY ARE REFRIGERATED.

. . . .

THE FLASHES OF LIGHT WHEN YOU RUB YOUR EYES ARE CALLED PHOSPHENES.

. . . .

WITHIN 20 SECONDS, ONE RED BLOOD CELLS WOULD HAVE ALREADY COMPLETED ONE LAP AROUND YOUR CIRCULATORY SYSTEM.

KANGAROOS NEVER STOP GROWING. FROM BIRTH, THEY WILL CONTINUE TO GROW UNTIL THEY PASS AWAY.

....

PEOPLE ONCE BELIEVED THAT CHEWING ON TREE BARK WILL KEEP YOUR GUMS HEALTHY.

....

THE INSECT POPULATION OF THE WORLD IS 1 BILLION TIMES MORE THAN THE WORLD POPULATION.

STUDIES INDICATE THAT NEGATIVE EMOTIONS LEAD TO LOWERED IMMUNE RESPONSES AGAINST DISEASES.

. . . .

THE HUMAN BRAIN USES 20 PERCENT OF THE OXYGEN IN YOUR BODY.

. . . .

ONE OF THE CLEANEST DOG BREEDS IN THE WORLD ARE POODLES. THEY DO NOT EXCESSIVELY MOLT.

OWLS HAVE SPECIALIZED FEATHERS WHICH MAKE THEM DEADLY HUNTERS AT NIGHT.

....

TANNING BEDS AND LAMPS INCREASE YOUR RISK OF DEVELOPING SKIN CANCER.

....

DESPITE THEIR APPEARANCE, PITBULLS ARE RANKED AS THE MOST AFFECTIONATE AND LEAST AGGRESSIVE BREED OF DOGS.

CHINA HAS A SERIES OF UNDERGROUND TUNNELS FOR TRANSPORTING BALLISTIC MISSILES.

· ·

WHEN THE TITANIC SANK IN 1912, THREE DOGS WERE ABLE TO SURVIVE.

· ·

A BRITISH SCIENTIST STUDYING CHOCOLATE HAD HER TASTE BUDS INSURED FOR 1 MILLION BRITISH POUNDS.

EMINEM'S 'RAP GOD' HOLDS THE WORLD RECORD FOR THE MOST WORDS IN A HIT SINGLE.

....

BLACK CAT APPRECIATION DAY IS CELEBRATED EVERY 17TH OF AUGUST.

....

MULTIPLYING 1089 BY 9 WILL GIVE YOU THE SAME NUMBERS IN REVERSE ORDER.

YOU CAN FIT ABOUT 400 GRAPEVINES IN ONE ACRE OF LAND. THIS IS EQUIVALENT TO ALMOST 5 TONS OF GRAPES!

....

THE LARGEST LIVING THING ON EARTH IS A GIANT SEQUOIA TREE CALLED 'GENERAL SHERMAN'.

....

THE PAINT ON THE EIFFEL TOWER IS EQUIVALENT TO TEN ELEPHANTS.

THE MAP SIZE IN GRAND THEFT AUTO V IS TWICE THE ACTUAL SIZE OF MANHATTAN.

....

THE QUEENS IN ANT COLONIES CAN LIVE UP TO AROUND THIRTY YEARS.

....

A TIME-ANXIOUS PERSON IS ONE WHO IS PERPETUALLY AFRAID OF BEING LATE.

THE EARTH HOLDS ABOUT 11 QUINTILLION POUNDS OF AIR.

· ·

THERE ARE OVER 6,000 SPECIES OF GRASS. THE MOST COMMON KINDS INCLUDE RICE, WHEAT, OATS, AND SUGARGANES.

· ·

APPLYING EQUAL PRESSURE TO ALL "SIDES" OF AN EGG WILL PREVENT IT FROM BREAKING.

A RHOMBICUBOCTAHEDRON IS A SHAPE WITH 26 SIDES.

· ·

IT TAKES URANUS 84 YEARS TO ORBIT THE SUN. ONE ROTATION ON THE SAME PLANET IS AROUND 17 HOURS LONG.

· ·

GARLIC IS KNOWN TO ATTRACT LEECHES.

ENGLAND AND PORTUGAL
MAINTAINS THE LONGEST
UNBROKEN ALLIANCE IN
WORLD HISTORY.

....

SLAVERY WAS LEGAL IN
MAURITANIA UNTIL 2007.
HOWEVER, 1-4 PERCENT OF
THE POPULATION STILL
LIVE AS SLAVES WITHIN ITS
BORDERS.

....

THE AVERAGE HORSE IS
CAPABLE OF 746 WATTS
OF POWER.

THE LEANING TOWER OF PISA IS TILTED DUE TO THE SOIL AT ITS BASE.

· ·

THE ONLY INNATE FEAR WE HAVE AT BIRTH IS THE FEAR OF FALLING AND OF LOUD NOISES.

· ·

THE GREAT PYRAMID OF GIZA HAS MORE A TOTAL OF 8 SIDES, DOUBLE THE NORMAL FOR MOST PYRAMIDS.

THE BRITISH POUND, THE WORLD'S OLDEST CURRENCY, DATES OVER 1,200 YEARS OLD IN USAGE.

....

RUSSELL HORNING IS FAMOUS ON THE INTERNET AS THE BACKPACK KID.

....

MOUNT EVEREST IS NOT THE TALLEST MOUNTAIN IN OUR SOLAR SYSTEM. THE OLYMPUS MONS IS.

THE DAY AFTER THANKSGIVING IS KNOWN BY MANY AMERICAN PLUMBERS AS "BROWN FRIDAY".

....

ADDING ALL THE NUMBERS ON A ROULETTE WHEEL WILL EQUAL TO 666,

....

THERE WERE LEMURS BEFORE THAT WERE THE SIZE OF GORILLAS! SADLY, THEY ARE NOW EXTINCT.

RUSSIANS BELIEVE THAT EATING ICE CREAM WILL KEEP THE BODY WARM.

· ·

CONNECTICUT ACCIDENTALLY ISSUED AN EMERGENCY EVACUATION ALERT IN 2005.

· ·

THE HUMAN VAGINA ALWAYS HOLDS A SMALL AMOUNT OF YEAST.

THE MONA LISA WAS STOLEN FROM THE LOUVRE MUSEUM IN 1911.

....

BI-WEEKLY HAS TWO CONNOTATIONS: IT CAN EITHER BE EVERY TWO WEEKS OR TWICE A WEEK.

....

THERAPY HAS BEEN FOUND TO BE LEAST EFFECTIVE AT BATTLING DEPRESSION COMPARED TO PLAYING VIDEO GAMES.

THERE ARE MORE POSSIBLE ARRANGEMENTS IN SHUFFLING A DECK OF CARDS THAN THERE ARE STARS IN THE SKY.

....

KITTENS WILL MEOW TO ITS MOTHER, BUT MORE FREQUENTLY TO HUMANS AS IT MATURES.

....

YOU ARE ABLE TO BECOME LESS DEPRESSED IF YOU STAY UP LONGER.

ACCORDING TO STUDIES, SEEING A POLAR BEAR DIRECTLY ATTACK ITS PREY IS CONSIDERED RARE.

· ·

IN 1927, THE U.S. GOVERNMENT ISSUED SANTA CLAUS A PILOT'S LICENSE.

· ·

GECKOS EAT THE SKIN THEY SHED TO PREVENT PREDATORS FROM FINDING THEM.

'SAMSUNG' TRANSLATES TO 'THREE STARS' IN THE KOREAN LANGUAGE.

· ·

IT DID NOT TAKE MORE THAN A MILLION DOLLARS TO BUILD THE MT. RUSHMORE MONUMENT.

· ·

THE MOST "MATHEMATICAL" FLAG IN THE WORLD BELONGS TO NEPAL.

IF YOU WERE TO CUT A STARFISH'S LEG, BLOOD WILL NOT SPILL OUT.

....

IN 1930, A BBC RADIO ANNOUNCER ONCE STATED THAT THEY DID NOT HAVE ANY NEWS TO ANNOUNCE.

....

MEXICAN PRISONS DO NOT PUNISH YOU FOR NON-VIOLENT ATTEMPTS TO ESCAPE.

THE RELEASE OF
POKEMON GO INCREASED
GAME-RELATED
ACCIDENTS BY 26.5
PERCENT.

· ·

SOURTOE COCKTAILS
ARE SERVED IN YUKON.
IT IS SERVED WITH A
HUMAN TOE FLOATING
INSIDE THE GLASS.

· ·

ENGLISH IS THE MOST
SPOKEN LANGUAGE IN
IRELAND.

THE HAPPIEST COUNTRIES IN THE WORLD HAVE THE HIGHEST ANTIDEPRESSANT CONSUMERS.

....

EVERY TEN YEARS, BRAIN FIBERS LOSE 10 PERCENT OF THEIR STRENGTH.

....

'TSUNDOKU' IS THE JAPANESE WORD FOR BOOK HOARDERS.

MINNESOTA HAS THE WORLD'S QUIETEST ROOM. THE NOISE IN THIS ROOM IS MEASURED IN NEGATIVE DECIBELS!

· ·

SHAKIRA WAS REJECTED FROM HER ELEMENTARY CHOIR GROUP.

· ·

12 PLANTS AND 5 ANIMALS MAKE UP 75 PERCENT OF DIETS AROUND THE WORLD.

AROUND 50 PERCENT OF THE MINED GOLD ON EARTH COMES FROM WITWATERSRAND IN SOUTH AFRICA.

....

PLANET X WAS RENAMED TO PLUTO THANKS TO AN 11 YEAR OLD GIRL.

....

THE FIRST SERVICE ANIMALS WERE ESTABLISHED IN GERMANY.

THE CORRECT ENGLISH TRANSLATION FOR JESUS FROM THE HEBREW 'YESHUA' IS 'JOSHUA'.

....

THE BOSS IN METAL GEAR SOLID 3 TAKES A WEEK TO BEAT.

....

JACK DANIELS, FOUNDER OF THE INFAMOUS WHISKEY, DIED FROM A TOE INJURY.

THE SPIKED DOG COLLARS ARE MEANT TO PROTECT THE DOGS' NECKS FROM ATTACKS.

· ·

THE 1996 FILM 'SCREAM' INCREASED THE USE OF CALLER I.D.'S IN THE UNITED STATES.

· ·

A POLISH DOCTOR ONCE FAKED A TYPHUS OUTBREAK TO KEEP THE NAZIS AWAY.

THE LARGEST GRAND PIANO IN THE WORLD WAS BUILT BY A TEENAGER IN NEW ZEALAND.

....

THE LARGEST PRIME NUMBER HAS 17,425,170 DIGITS.

....

A JOCKEY FROM 1923 MANAGED TO FINISH A RACE AFTER DYING FROM A HEART ATTACK.

THE FAT BUDDHA STATUE
AND THE ONE IN PICTURES
IS NOT BUDDHA HIMSELF.

· ·

POINTING YOUR CAR
KEYS TO YOUR HEAD
HELPS YOU FIND YOUR
CAR FASTER.

· ·

A SINGLE STRAND OF
SPAGHETTI IS
INDIVIDUALLY REFERRED
TO AS SPAGHETTO.

THE TERM 'SHOTGUN' FOR THE FRONT PASSENGER SEAT COMES FROM A MESSENGER.

· ·

THE LETTER 'J' IS THE ONLY LETTER IN THE ENGLISH ALPHABET WHICH CANNOT BE FOUND ON THE PERIODIC TABLE.

· ·

ABOUT $3.70 IS GIVEN TO AN AMERICAN CHILD PER TOOTH THEY LOSE.

THE SCIENTIFIC TERM FOR BRAIN FREEZE IS SPHENOPALATINE GANGLION NEURALGIA.

· ·

IN 1979-1999, PLUTO WAS ONCE TEMPORARILY CLOSER TO THE SUN THAN NEPTUNE.

· ·

BEN & JERRY'S HAS A GRAVEYARD FOR THEIR FORMER FLAVOURS.

ST. LUCIA IS THE ONLY COUNTRY THAT IS NAMED AFTER A WOMAN WHO WAS A CHRISTIAN MARTYR.

....

A COMMON SOUVENIR PEOPLE BRING FROM THE UNITED STATES ARE RED SOLO CUPS.

....

FLOSSING ONE'S TEETH REGULARLY CAN HELP IMPROVE MEMORY.

IF A BODY IS TOO OBESE, IT CAN CAUSE COMPLICATIONS WHEN BEING CREMATED.

. . . .

THE BACKWARD PUNCTUATION MARK IS USED TO SIGNIFY SARCASM.

. . . .

MICE TYPICALLY ONLY LIVE FOR 6 MONTHS IN THE WILD DUE TO PREDATORS.

THE AVERAGE 150-POUND PERSON CAN BURN 114 CALORIES AN HOUR JUST BY STANDING STILL.

· ·

THERE IS AN UNDERWATER VERSION OF RUGBY WHICH IS PLAYED IN REGULATION POOLS.

· ·

'DR PEPPER' DOES NOT HAVE A PERIOD IN ITS NAME.

PEOPLE WHO POST THEIR FITNESS ROUTINE ON SOCIAL MEDIA ARE MORE LIKELY TO HAVE PSYCHOLOGICAL PROBLEMS.

· ·

IT IS ILLEGAL TO DIE IN SVALBARD ISLAND, NORWAY.

· ·

STEPHEN HAWKING HELD A RECEPTION FOR TIME TRAVELERS IN 2009.

IKEA ACTUALLY STANDS FOR 'INGVAR KAMPRAD ELMTARYD AGUNNARYD', THE NAME OF THE COMPANY'S OWNER.

· ·

VIOLIN BOWS ARE MADE FROM HORSEHAIR.

· ·

THE HAPPIEST PRISONER ON DEATH ROW HAD AN IQ OF 46. IT WAS THEN LATER FOUND OUT THAT HE WAS INNOCENT.

HONEYBEES CAN
RECOGNIZE HUMAN FACES.

· ·

FACEBOOK, INSTAGRAM,
AND TWITTER ARE ALL
BANNED IN CHINA.
ANYONE CAUGHT USING
ANY OF THEM WHILE
INSIDE THE COUNTRY
CAN BE ARRESTED.

· ·

THE ANTARCTIC GLACIERS
ARE MADE UP OF 3
PERCENT PENGUIN URINE.

THE MAYO CLINIC MADE GLOW-IN-THE-DARK CATS WHILE TRYING TO FIND A CURE FOR AIDS.

· ·

95 PERCENT OF PEOPLE TEXT THINGS THEY WOULD NEVER SAY IN PERSON.

· ·

UP TO 20 PERCENT OF POWER OUTAGES IN THE U.S. ARE DUE TO SQUIRRELS.

THE PREMIERE OF THE TV REALITY SHOW '16 AND PREGNANT' HELPED LOWER THE RATE OF TEEN PREGNANCY.

· ·

BABY OCTOPI ARE THE SIZE OF A FLEA.

· ·

THERE IS A SPECIES OF SPIDER DUBBED AS THE 'HOBO SPIDER'. THESE SPIDERS ARE NOT DEADLY.

THE U.S. NAVY USES XBOX CONTROLLERS FOR THEIR PERISCOPES.

....

THE AVERAGE MALE WILL BECOME BORED AFTER 26 MINUTES OF SHOPPING.

....

THE ROAR OF A LION IS ABOUT 114 DECIBELS AND CAN BE HEARD UP TO 5 MILES AWAY!

A PALINDROME IS A SENTENCE THAT IS THE SAME WHEN READ FORWARDS AND BACKWARDS.

· ·

BABY SPIDERS ARE OFFICIALLY CALLED 'SPIDERLINGS'.

· ·

AN EAGLE IS CAPABLE OF KILLING A YOUNG DEER AND FLYING AWAY WITH IT.

RAVENS ARE ALWAYS AWARE WHEN SOMEONE IS WATCHING THEM.

. . . .

SCHOOLMASTER IS AN OLDER TERM USED TO REFER TO A MALE TEACHER.

. . . .

MORE MONOPOLY MONEY IS PRINTED ANNUALLY RATHER THAN ACTUAL CURRENCY.

SLOTHS CAN HOLD THEIR
BREATH UNDERWATER
FOR UP TO 40 MINUTES

· ·

A 2018 SURVEY SHOWED
THAT 60 PERCENT OF
MILLENNIALS GO TO
SLEEP NAKED.

· ·

THE CHICKEN IS THE
CLOSEST RELATIVE TO
THE T-REX.

A NASA EXPERIMENT REVEALED THAT SPACE TRAVEL MAKES MICE RUN IN CIRCLES AND NO ONE KNOWS EXACTLY WHY.

· ·

EVEN THOUGH THEY HAVE SIX LEGS, DRAGONFLIES CAN'T WALK.

· ·

BASENJI DOGS ARE THE ONLY BREED OF DOGS THAT CANNOT BARK.

MULTI-COLOR FURRED SQUIRRELS ROAM THE LANDS OF SOUTHERN INDIA.

· ·

THE AVERAGE AMERICAN ANNUALLY SPENDS 2.5 DAYS LOOKING FOR LOST THINGS.

· ·

THE MOST COMMONLY USED PASSWORD IS 123456.

OPTICAL ILLUSIONS CAN BE FOUND AT THE SEA FLOOR, LIKE A SMALL LAKE-LIKE POOL THAT WAS UPSIDE DOWN!

· ·

QUEEN ELIZABETH IS A TRAINED MECHANIC!

· ·

TED HASTINGS CURRENTLY HOLDS THE RECORD OF PUTTING ON OVER 260 T-SHIRTS.

VANTABLACK, THE WORLD'S DARKEST SHADE OF BLACK, HAS A TRADEMARK.

. . . .

IN SOUTH AMERICA AND SOME TROPICAL ISLANDS, ORANGES ARE GREEN ALL YEAR ROUND!

. . . .

ALASKA IS THE ONLY U.S. STATE WHOSE NAME IS ON A SINGLE ROW ON THE KEYBOARD.

SWISS MORTALITY STATISTICS SHOW THAT YOU ARE 13.8 PERCENT MORE LIKELY TO DIE ON YOUR DATE OF BIRTH.

....

PINOCCHIO SAYING "MY NOSE WILL GROW NOW" WOULD CREATE A PARADOX.

....

AMONG ALL THE DISNEY PRINCESSES, MULAN HAS THE HIGHEST KILL COUNT.

'TRAILERS' WERE FIRST INTRODUCED DURING THE 1910'S ARE WERE ORIGINALLY SHOWN AFTER THE MOVIE.

· ·

BILLY GOATS URINATE ON THEIR HEADS TO BECOME MORE ATTRACTIVE.

· ·

PLAYING DANCE MUSIC HELPS KEEP MOSQUITOES AWAY.

BACK IN THE 1800'S, PEOPLE USED TO ANSWER THE PHONE WITH "AHOY!".

....

ONLY ONE STATE CAPITAL IN THE U.S. HAS NO MCDONALD'S... THAT IS MONTPELIER, VERMONT.

....

FRIGATE BIRDS CAN SLEEP WHILE FLYING.

SEEDS OF APPLES,
APRICOT, CHERRY, AND
PEACH CONTAIN CYANIDE.

· ·

THE FINGERNAILS ON A
PERSON'S DOMINANT HAND
GROW FASTER.

· ·

BECAUSE OF NEGATIVE
GEOTROPISM, BANANAS
GET THEIR CURVED
SHAPE BY GROWING
TOWARDS THE SUN.

CATS DON'T HAVE THE BASE PAIR OF GENES THAT DETECT SWEET FLAVORS.

··

AROUND 7 PERCENT OF AMERICANS BELIEVE THAT CHOCOLATE MILK COMES FROM BROWN COWS.

··

THE AVERAGE ADULT SPENDS MORE TIME IN THE LOO THAN EXERCISING.

THE METAL STUDS ON DENIM JEANS ACT AS A SUPPORT FOR THE CLOTH AND MAKE THE JEANS MORE DURABLE.

· ·

THE OPPOSITE SIDES OF DICE WILL ALWAYS EQUAL TO SEVEN.

· ·

IN EUROPE AND THE U.S., MAY 29TH IS PUT A PILLOW ON YOUR FRIDGE DAY.

THE ONLY ENGLISH WORD THAT ENDS WITH 'MT" IS DREAMT.

. . . .

SMALLPOX AND RINDERPEST ARE THE ONLY TWO DISEASES THAT HAVE BEEN COMPLETELY ERADICATED.

. . . .

THE KING OF HEARTS IS THE ONLY KING WITHOUT A MUSTACHE.

STUDIES SHOW THAT MOST SNAKE SPECIES CAN DETECT EARTHQUAKES BEFORE THEY OCCUR.

· ·

BABY SEA OTTERS ARE INCAPABLE OF SWIMMING ON THEIR OWN.

· ·

A SINGLE DOLLAR BILL COSTS 5 CENTS TO MAKE.

THE FEAR OF THE NUMBER 13 IS CALLED 'TRISKAIDEKAPHOBIA'.

· ·

THE NORTHERN CARDINAL HAS BEEN VOTED AS THE MOST POPULAR STATE BIRD IN THE U.S.

· ·

NO TWO TEETH FROM DIFFERENT PEOPLE WILL EVER BE ALIKE.

GUYANA'S KAIETEUR FALLS IS THE LARGEST SINGLE DROP WATERFALL IN THE WORLD.

. . . .

LACK OF SLEEP MAKES IT HARDER FOR PEOPLE TO LOSE WEIGHT.

. . . .

MORE PEOPLE SPEAK ENGLISH AS THEIR SECOND LANGUAGE THAN THOSE WHO USE IT AS THEIR NATIVE TONGUE.

DRIVING SOUTH FROM DETROIT WILL LEAD TO CANADA.

· ·

THE ODDS OF GETTING A ROYAL FLUSH IS 1 IN 649,740.

· ·

NEIL ARMSTRONG NEVER SAID "THAT'S ONE SMALL STEP FOR MAN".

DEPENDING ON HOW THEY
DESCEND, WATERFALLS
CAN BE CLASSIFIED INTO
10 MAIN CATEGORIES.

· ·

CACTUS SPINES CAN BE
USED TO MAKE HOOKS,
NEEDLES, AND COMBS!

· ·

THE FOLDS IN THE
CHEF'S HAT
REPRESENTS THE
NUMBER OF WAYS YOU
CAN COOK AN EGG.

SOME RECORDS SHOW THAT WHEN WOMEN LOSE WEIGHT, THEIR MEMORY IMPROVES.

....

HARRIET, CHARLES DARWIN'S PET TURTLE, OUTLIVED HIM. IT WAS 176 YEARS OLD BY THE TIME IT PASSED AWAY.

....

AROUND 30,000 RUBBER DUCKS WERE LOST AT SEA IN 1992.

ONE ANT SPECIES CAN ONLY BE FOUND IN MANHATTAN, NEW YORK.

· ·

RESEARCH FOUND THAT DOLPHINS USE THEIR UNIQUE VOCAL WHISTLES TO IDENTIFY AND DIFFERENTIATE ONE ANOTHER.

· ·

THE INVENTOR OF FRISBEE BECAME A FRISBEE HIMSELF!

CACTI COME IN MANY
DIFFERENT COLOURS
OTHER THAN GREEN.

....

A CHINESE PANDA ONCE
FAKED A PREGNANCY TO
GET BETTER HEALTHCARE
AND ATTENTION FROM
THE ZOOKEEPERS.

....

THE WORLD'S LARGEST
PYRAMID IS FOUND IN
CHOLULA, MEXICO.

SALIVA CAN BE USED TO MONITOR ALCOHOL INTAKE, SMOKING, AND DRUG USE.

· ·

A MAN WAS ONCE SAVED BY A SEA LION FROM DROWNING, AFTER A FAILED SUICIDE ATTEMPT WHICH BROKE HIS BACK.

· ·

RESEARCH SHOWS THAT CANINES HAVE AN 85 PERCENT SUCCESS RATE WHEN HUNTING.

MILK WAGONS ARE THE REASON WHY WE HAVE ROADWAY LINES.

· ·

THE BASEBALL HALL OF FAME ONCE HAD AN UNAUTHORIZED INDUCTEE WHICH TOOK 6 YEARS BEFORE BEING DISCOVERED!

· ·

THE KKK WAS TAKEN DOWN WITH THE HELP OF SUPERMAN.

THE WORLD'S MOST SUCCESSFUL PIRATE WAS A CHINESE WOMAN NAMED CHING SHIH.

....

MOST BUSINESSES DO NOT SEE THE PRACTICALITY OF HAVING DIAPER TABLES.

....

THE WEALTHY IN RUSSIA HIRE FAKE 'AMBULANCES' TO FACILITATE FASTER TRAVEL AT $200 AN HOUR.

THE STATE OF VIRGINIA
MAY CONTAIN HIDDEN
TREASURE, ACCORDING TO
THE BEALE CIPHERS.

· ·

MONTY PYTHON HAS ONE
OF THE MOST REQUESTED
SONGS FOR FUNERALS IN
ENGLAND.

· ·

THE INCAS PRIMARILY
USED KNOTS TO KEEP
TRACK OF RECORDS.

BY ROYAL LAW, QUEEN ELIZABETH IS NOT ALLOWED TO SIT UPON A FOREIGN THRONE.

· ·

DUE TO THE FIREWORKS, MANY PETS IN THE UNITED STATES RUN AWAY ON JULY 4TH.

· ·

THE BOTTLE OF A BOTTLED WATER HAS AN EXPIRATION DATE.

TIMOTHY LEARY ESCAPED BY SIMPLY WALKING AWAY FROM THE MINIMUM-SECURITY PRISON HE WAS IN.

....

THE STORY OF BEAUTY AND THE BEAST WAS AIMED TO MAKE WOMEN OPEN TO ARRANGED MARRIAGES.

....

THE FEDORA WAS ORIGINALLY MADE FOR WOMEN.

AN AMERICAN PARK
RANGER WAS HIT BY
LIGHTNING 7 TIMES,
EARNING HIM THE NAME
"HUMAN LIGHTING ROD".

· ·

DAVID BOWIE'S HEROES
PERFORMANCE HELPED
TOPPLE THE BERLIN WALL.

· ·

COLD WATER IS JUST AS
CLEANSING AS HOT
WATER.

75 BURGERS ARE SOLD IN MCDONALD'S EVERY SECOND.

....

MOMS IN DENMARK ARE KNOWN TO BE THE MOST HARDWORKING MOMS IN THE WORLD.

....

AN ENCRYPTED MONUMENT STANDS OUTSIDE OF THE CIA HEADQUARTERS IN VIRGINIA.

SEARS ONCE OFFERED KIT HOUSES THAT YOU WOULD HAVE TO ASSEMBLE YOURSELF.

· ·

'KUMMERSPECK' IS A GERMAN TERM FOR THE WEIGHT GAINED FROM EMOTIONAL EATING.

· ·

IOANNIS IKONOMOU HAS BEEN THE CHIEF TRANSLATOR OF THE EUROPEAN PARLIAMENT SINCE 2002.

ALAN SHEPARD IS THE ONE AND ONLY PERSON TO HAVE PLAYED ON THE MOON.

....

SOMEONE WILL WRITE AND RECITE A POEM AT YOUR FUNERAL IF YOUR DIE IN THE NETHERLANDS.

....

THE LARGEST LIVING ORGANISM IS AN ASPEN GROVE REFERRED TO AS 'PANDO'.

FLIPPING A SHARK OVER WILL RENDER IT TEMPORARILY IMMOBILE DUE TO SHOCK.

. . . .

BLACK TAXIS IN LONDON ARE TALL SO THAT MEN WILL BE ABLE TO RIDE THEM WITHOUT REMOVING THEIR TOP HATS.

. . . .

A PISTOL CAN ONLY BE USED BY ONE HAND.

MALE STUDENTS ATTENDING BRIGHAM YOUNG UNIVERSITY CANNOT GROW BEARDS.

....

MELTING GLACIERS MAKE FIZZY NOISES KNOWN AS 'BERGY SELTZER' BECAUSE THEY SOUND SIMILAR TO FIZZING SODA.

....

TEACHERS IN NORTH KOREA WERE ONCE REQUIRED TO PLAY THE ACCORDION.

THE FLAMING HOT CHEETOS ACTUALLY CAME FROM THE IDEA OF A JANITOR. HE IS NOW A PEPSICO EXECUTIVE.

....

SOME SAILORS USE BLACK CATS AS THE SHIP'S CAT IN HOPES OF A SAFE VOYAGE.

....

'OMG' WAS FIRST USED IN A LETTER TO WINSTON CHURCHILL IN 1917.

AMERICAN AIRLINES SAVED MONEY BY GETTING RID OF OLIVES FROM THEIR MEALS.

....

MCDONALD'S ONCE HAD BUBBLEGUM-FLAVOURED BROCCOLI SUPPOSEDLY TO MAKE KIDS ENJOY VEGETABLES.

....

THE LARGEST RECORDED SNOWFLAKE IS 15 INCHES WIDE.

IN 1992, BRITAIN
LAUNCHED A HOTLINE
WHERE PEOPLE CAN
REPORT ROGUE TRAFFIC
CONES.

· ·

A MAN IN FLORIDA ONCE
THREW A LIVE ALLIGATOR
THROUGH A DRIVE-THRU
WINDOW AT WENDY'S.

· ·

OWNING ONLY 1 GUINEA
PIG IS ILLEGAL IN
SWITZERLAND.

THE PUNCTUATION '?!' IS CALLED AN INTERROBANG. IT WAS INVENTED DURING THE 1960'S.

....

DURING THE VICTORIAN ERA, LEECHES WERE USED TO PREDICT THE WEATHER.

....

A CITY IN OREGON IS CALLED BORING, WHICH WAS NAMED AFTER ITS FOUNDER.

IN 2006, NEW ZEALAND WAS AUCTIONED ON EBAY BY AN AUSTRALIAN MAN WITH A STARTING BID OF $0.01.

······························

THERE ARE MORE THAN 200 FLAVOURS OF KIT KAT IN JAPAN.

······························

SCOTLAND HAS OVER 400 WORDS TO REFER TO SNOW!

DUE TO THE SIMILARITY OF THEIR SPIKY OUTER SKIN, PINEAPPLES HAVE BEEN NAMED AFTER PINECONES.

· ·

A FRENCH PIG WAS ONCE JAILED AND EXECUTED FOR THE 'MURDER' OF A CHILD.

· ·

A PERSON'S FUNNY BONE IS ACTUALLY A NERVE.

THE BONES OF THE HUMAN BODY CAN MULTIPLY IN DENSITY. BUT THIS OCCURS ONLY IN VERY EXTREME CASES.

. . . .

THE SOUND FROM 'CRACKLING' YOUR KNUCKLES ARE ACTUALLY CAUSED BY THE GASSES BEING RELEASED FROM THE JOINTS.

. . . .

APPLE ONCE HAD A CLOTHING LINE.

3 MUSKETEER CHOCOLATE BARS USED TO HAVE 3 FLAVORS: STRAWBERRY, CHOCOLATE, AND VANILLA.

••••••••••••••••••••••••••••••

THERE WAS A FIFTH MEMBER OF THE BEATLES WHO DIED DUE TO A BRAIN HEMORRHAGE BEFORE THE BAND CAME INTO FAME.

••••••••••••••••••••••••••••••

THE SALTY TASTE OF BACON IS NOT NATURAL.

AURORA AUSTRALIS IS THE SISTER PHENOMENON OF AURORA BOREALIS. IT CAN BE VIEWED IN THE SOUTHERN HEMISPHERE.

....

CROCODILES ARE ONE OF EARTH'S OLDEST LIVING CREATURES.

....

THE MOST WIDELY PRINTED BOOK IN THE WORLD IS THE CATALOG FOR IKEA.

CAP'N CRUNCH'S FULL NAME IS HORATIO MAGELLAN CRUNCH. HE WAS NAMED AFTER THE FERDINAND MAGELLAN.

· ·

CAP'N CRUNCH WAS ONCE SUED FOR NOT USING REAL BERRIES.

· ·

ON AVERAGE, INDIANS SPEND 10 HOURS MORE OF THEIR TIME DURING THE WEEK JUST READING.

BECAUSE OF HIGH TEMPERATURES DURING A RACE, NASCAR DRIVERS CAN LOSE UP TO 10 POUNDS OF WEIGHT BY SWEATING.

· ·

THE CHILDREN'S BOOK AUTHOR ROALD DAHL WAS ACTUALLY A SPY.

· ·

ONE STRAND OF HAIR CAN HOLD UP TO 3 OUNCES OF WEIGHT.

Printed in Great Britain
by Amazon